Live Tax Free in Canada

by
Adam Starchild

Books for Business
New York - Hong Kong

Live Tax Free in Canada

by
Adam Starchild

ISBN: 0-89499-204-X

Books for Business
New York - Hong Kong
http://www.BusinessBooksInternational.com

Contents

Immigrate to Canada - Leave Taxes Behind

Introduction

At the outset we warn you the tax reduction suggestions contained in this exclusive report may sound radical to the less adventurous reader. However drastic, you can be certain the steps recommended here are legal and the ultimate financial goals attainable - for those willing to do what is necessary.

The rewards for the bold and brave include five years free of tax obligations - and much lower taxes in the years beyond. The sacrifice required may be the renunciation of your United States citizenship, but in exchange you get the solid prospect of a lifetime with little or no taxes - with assured protection for your assets - and with expanded future income and accumulated personal wealth.

The key to this almost tax-free existence is found in the right combination of exceptional Canadian statutory tax breaks available right now for new immigrants - together with your own careful structuring of personal, corporate and family finances on an international scale.

Read on and discover a whole new concept of tax saving and asset protection, perhaps not for the faint-hearted - but certainly for the wise and wealthy.

Canada - Number One in the World

In 1992 when leading economists at United Nations headquarters in New York researched and published an international guide to the best nations in which to live and work, Canada was judged "number one." (Japan came in second, the United States only sixth and in tenth place was merry olde England).

The factors used in making this surprising choice (to Americans, perhaps) encompassed Canada's high standard of living; minimal class divisions; low crime rates with a high sense of individual personal security; the clean environment, air and water; beautiful scenery and wide open spaces; many and varied economic opportunities; ample government support services; extensive infrastructure; comprehensive shopping and sports facilities; available and affordable housing; and the generous hospitality of the Canadian people.

Even with long harsh winters, a continuing bi-lingual, English-French problem and long-standing separatist political sentiment in the province of Quebec, on balance the UN officials found Canada to be the most attractive nation in the world.

The virtues of Canada as the place to live are known around the world, if the number of recent immigrants is any indicator. In 1993, for example, Canada's population of 29.2 million - projected to peak at about 31 million by 2026 - was increased by 240,138 new citizens. Canada, a modern nation built by European settlers, has increased its flow of immigrants by three-fold since 1985, a year when total population was 25 million and only 85,000 new citizens arrived. Since then increasing numbers have been admitted including many wealthy Asians, especially residents of Hong Kong, the British crown colony slated for Communist China's take over in 1997. The top ten national sources of immigrants since 1986 have been the United States, India, Vietnam, Poland, the United Kingdom, the Philippines, Guyana, and El Salvador.

Canada now has the highest per capita immigration rate of any industrialized nation in the world, an in-flux that has caused widespread public demand for limiting further immigration. A May 1995 national poll showed three out of five Canadians favoring a five-year moratorium on all new immigration.

Reflecting the trend towards tough new immigration controls in most western European nations - and similar demands in the U.S. -

Canada's government adopted a scaled-down 1995 immigration quota in the range of 190,00 to 215,000, well below recent annual quotas of 230,000.

But don't let this anti-immigration sentiment concern you. As you will learn in a moment, you may qualify as just the type of new citizen Canada welcomes with open arms.

Tax Free New Canadians

About Canadian Taxes

Before we get to the good news - the big tax break for new Canadian immigrants - you should know that the tax system of Canada is tough and comprehensive, imposing burdensome tax rates on the income of individual taxpayers (over 50 percent), and corporations (up to 45 percent). In 1994 writing in the *Wall Street Journal*, economist Alan Reynolds of the Hudson Institute in Indianapolis offered the opinion that "Canada is being taxed to death," citing high income and corporate taxes as well as a seven percent federal sales tax piled on top of similar provincial taxes.

But there is one very attractive feature of Canadian taxation policy; unlike the United States, Canada does not tax the worldwide income or foreign assets of its non-resident citizens living abroad. Canada taxes only the worldwide income of its residents - citizens and resident aliens alike - who live in Canada at any time during the calendar year. A "resident" by law includes individuals, corporations and trusts located in Canada.

Non-resident Canadians, wherever they live, are taxed on income sources within the country, and on business and other capital assets if taxable transactions occur within Canada. Canadian citizens employed abroad, even for extended periods of time, are liable for some limited domestic income taxes, though double taxation credits are permitted when foreign taxes are paid.

Enjoying Life Tax Free

However tough Canadian taxes may be for the average native-born citizen living in Canada's eleven provinces and two territories, there exists a huge loophole available only to wealthy new immigrants. This major tax saving

8

was deliberately written into law in order to encourage new arrivals with financial means.

And it is this Canadian preference for new citizens with substantial investment capital that can translate into huge tax savings and far-reaching financial gains for you and your business.

Here's why:

- A qualified immigrant accepted for eventual Canadian citizenship is eligible for a complete personal income tax moratorium for the first five calendar years of residence in Canada - zero taxes if the source of your income is an offshore, non-Canadian trust or corporation - either or both of which you can easily create before you move to Canada and become a citizen.

  As a general rule, Canada has a three year residence requirement after immigrant admission before citizenship is granted, but a five year residence is required in order to be eligible for this very special tax break.

- Canadian citizens and resident aliens employed by certain statutorily-recognized "international financial centers," such as the major one that has been developed in Montreal, are forgiven 50 percent of all federal and provincial income taxes as long as they are employed by one of the qualified companies that are a part of the center.

Generally combined federal/provincial income and social security taxes average one third of gross salary, so this specialized employment earns a substantial tax saving.

• Much "offshore" or foreign source income, dividends and interest paid to Canadian citizens, new or old, can be sheltered from immediate income or other taxes, especially if payments come from qualified foreign trusts or "affiliated corporations" as recognized by Canadian revenue laws.

• Unlike the U.S. with its top rate of 55 percent estate taxes, Canada has abolished all death taxes. The heirs of wealthy Americans with an estate of $3 million or more pay 55 percent of the estate value - and can pay as much as 60 percent in total U.S. federal death taxes. Even the estates of Americans who die leaving as little as $600,000 pay 37 percent in death taxes. State estate taxes and probate fees are added to these hefty U.S. sums.

In sharp contrast, Canadians pay no estate taxes. The federal estate tax was abolished in 1971, with the provinces following suit until the last death tax was repealed by Quebec in 1986.

- After the new Canadian citizen's five-year tax free residency, a Canadian who moves his or her residence to another country is taxed by Revenue Canada (their Internal Revenue Service) only on income earned or paid from within Canada - not on the person's worldwide income, a distinct tax advantage Americans living abroad do not enjoy.

However, a naturalized Canadian citizen who lives ten consecutive years or more outside Canada can be stripped of citizenship at the discretion of the government, a point to keep in mind when planning your future.

Consider This Scenario

Let's suppose a wealthy American citizen planning for the future wishes to sell an established business, or for that matter, convert fixed assets into liquid cash for investment or other purposes. Depending on how long the property has been held and how the liquidation deal is structured, the seller may face U.S. capital gains taxes at the current maximum rate of 38 percent.

Depending on the seller's tax bracket, increased income taxes can be 40 percent or more. In either case, a major part of the cash proceeds from the sale or conversion will be devoured by the U.S. Internal Revenue Service and state tax authorities before the seller ever sees a thin dime.

How can this enormous tax burden be avoided?

What if title to the U.S. business or assets is transferred to a foreign trust (with the property owner as the beneficiary) or to a corporation he or she controls, conveniently located in a low or no-tax offshore jurisdiction?

And what if, after the trust or corporation receives title, the former U.S. owner/donor applies for and receives Canadian citizenship, renounces U.S. citizenship and becomes a legal resident of Canada for at least five years?

That offshore trust or corporation will have a five-year period in which to pay benefits or income to the ex-U.S./new Canadian citizen - a free spirit who will have absolutely no income or capital gains tax liability in either the U.S. or Canada - if that intrepid person carefully follows every step required by the U.S. and Canadian laws that are available to accomplish this unique tax-free status.

It sounds to good to be true? Read on.

Becoming a Canadian

Interested Americans

For anyone interested in obtaining Canadian citizenship it is advisable to explore fully any possible family ties one may have to the country. The Canadian government is helpful in providing answers about whether a foreign national may be eligible by law for Canadian citizenship based on ancestry. Any Canadian consulate will provide a personal history information form to be completed and submitted with copies of relevant birth records to the Registrar of Canadian Citizenship in the capital city of Ottawa.

A "Certificate of Canadian Citizenship" is automatically issued to anyone who qualifies for citizenship by family descent, and this can serve as the least complicated basis on which to establish a new legal residence in Canada.

Maybe you would like to test personally the northern waters before making any major decision about a future in Canada. Fortunately, Americans thinking about immigrating can explore life north of the border for an extended period. Since 1989 the U.S.-Canadian Free Trade Agreement has allowed reciprocal extended stays of up to one year, with no requirement to obtain a special visa. Americans employed in certain occupations can enter, live and work in Canada without a permit and with no prior approval, and the number of one-year extensions is unlimited.

This right to work in Canada includes those Americans working for U.S. firms who do research and designing, purchasing, sales and contract negotiation, customs brokering, financial services, public relations, advertising, tourism and market research. It also includes professionals, so long as they are paid by a U.S. source.

As a general rule, Canada and the United States have the longest open border of any two neighboring nations in the world. Entry to either country requires no special visa or passport, only proper personal identification such as a state or provincial motor vehicle operators license or voters card. Tourists automatically are allowed to stay for at least 90 days without special permission.

One thing is certain - Americans and Canadians are no strangers to each other. U.S. investors own over 50 percent of all Canadian manufacturing and are the fourth largest investors in the total economy, after investors from Great Britain, the Netherlands and Japan. Overall, the U.S. has $73 billion invested in Canada and Canadians hold $51.2 billion in U.S. assets. The two nations have the largest bilateral volume of annual trade in the world; in 1994 it encompassed $100.4 billion in exports from the U.S., and $11.2 billion in Canadian exports to America.

Open Door for Immigrant Investors

Though there certainly is concern among Canadians about increased immigration, Canada keeps the official welcome mat out for skilled workers, professionals - and especially *for wealthy investors who wish to become Canadian citizens.*

Independent applicants for "permanent residence" - as Canadians call immigrant status - are rated on a point system that takes into account age, education, fluency in English and French, financial standing, occupational or professional experience, training and local demand for certain types of workers, geographic destination and a personal assessment of the applicant. Certain needed occupations are favored. Seventy points and up is passing.

The common method for prospective new immigrants is to obtain work from a Canadian employer in advance of an application for entry, or by applying for an immigrant visa with a job offer already in hand.

Completely separate from the point system for admissions, Canadian law favors as a special "independent class" certain preferred immigrants including investors, entrepreneurs, the self-employed and those who will add to the "cultural and artistic life" of the nation. With minor variation in the each of the provinces, investor-immigrants generally must have a net worth in excess of C$500,000 and be willing to invest at least C$250,000 in Canada for a minimum three-to-five year period.

With proof of sufficient assets and an attractive business plan, especially one creating new jobs for Canadians, an investor applicant's "permanent residence" and eventual citizenship is almost assured. Government loan guarantees and other assistance may be available for investors willing to invest larger sums of C$750,000 or more. This investor visa category has been heavily used by wealthy Hong Kong Chinese moving to Vancouver, now home to a large and influential Asian-Canadian community.

For potential investor visa applicants, the government rolls out the proverbial "red carpet," officially known as the "Business Migration Programme." Business experience, marketing skills, contacts within Canada and an adequate credit rating and available funds all greatly increase this type of applicant's chance of success.

Applicants are usually required to submit detailed business proposals or general business plans, which must accompany the application for permanent residence. Such plans must detail the nature of the business, operating procedures, key personnel (which may just be the applicant), marketing and a financial plan. As in the U.S., the usual forms for business in Canada include the sole proprietorship, general and limited partnerships and corporations.

Canadian Immigration Process

There you receive an "Immigration Questionnaire" requiring basic personal information about you, your spouse and family. Once this is submitted and checked, within a few weeks a more detailed questionnaire will be presented if the applicant is found initially acceptable. After this second document is reviewed, a personal interview is required and then, medical examinations for the applicant, spouse and family will be needed.

If all goes well, shortly thereafter you will receive a visa for entry into Canada as a landed immigrant: "Welcome, bien venue a Canada."

It is worth noting that Canada recognizes the principle of dual nationality, allowing successful applicants for citizenship to retain their nationality of origin. For reasons that will become obvious in a moment, that choice is not a viable option for an ex-American becoming a Canadian citizen in order to obtain the five-year tax relief the law offers.

Another advantage that comes with this new citizenship is the international official acceptance of the Canadian passport, one of the most respected in the world.

The Big Change - U.S. Expatriation

Later we'll describe more fully the amazing potential tax savings that await you north of the border, but first let's face the hard realities essential to make this tax free plan work for a willing new Canadian immigrant.

The potential immigrant from America will have to give up United States citizenship, formally renouncing his or her U.S. status in a way that carefully avoids identifying the purpose as avoidance of U.S. taxes - otherwise the IRS will pursue you and any U.S. income or assets you may have. (For the record, fewer than a thousand Americans renounce their citizenship each year).

Goodbye to the IRS

Under current U.S. law (section 877 of the Foreign Investors Tax Act of 1966) a citizen who is suspected of giving up U.S. citizenship for "the principal purpose" of avoiding taxes can still be taxed on U.S. source income for up to ten years after leaving the country, and if he or she dies in that period, the IRS can go after the assets in the estate still located in the U.S. or any payments made to U.S. beneficiaries and heirs of the decedent's estate.

However, don't get too nervous. The truth is - this law leaks like a sieve because American expatriates, long before renouncing U.S. citizenship, routinely restructure their assets, sending wealth abroad to avoid the grasp of the IRS. The U.S. Treasury openly admits monitoring of such subjective private transactions is all but impossible. And this difficulty of proof of intentions is why the recent debate in Congress about a proposed "expatriation tax" on unrealized capital gains is so much political hot air. By the time someone at IRS figures out an expatriation tax might be due, the person is long gone from the United States - along with his or her liquid assets and wealth.

Do It the Right Way

Here's how expatriation from the U.S. can be accomplished, while avoiding pitfalls along the way:

It is crucial to obtain proper legal advice on expatriation in order to be effective in renouncing citizenship. The worst case is to wind up in an ambiguous dual national status with U.S. citizenship retained and a new citizenship added - you then may find yourself within the potential grasp of two government taxing authorities.

Generally, an ex-American who properly renounces citizenship is treated by U.S. law as a non-resident alien, taxable at a flat 30 percent rate only on certain types of passive income derived from U.S. sources, and on net profits of the sale of a U.S. trade or business at regular graduated rates. Such a person can usually safely spend only about 122 days a year within the United States, before exposing themselves to IRS claims for full U.S. taxation based on alien residency risked by a longer stay.

Remember, the U.S. is one of the few countries that imposes income and estate taxes on its citizens on their worldwide income and assets, regardless of where the person is a resident or where those assets are located. That's exactly why Canadian citizenship can be so valuable to an ex-American - Revenue Canada doesn't tax worldwide income of citizens living abroad like the IRS does for Americans.

Another strict caution: you must be certain to obtain valid Canadian citizenship **before** you renounce your U.S. citizenship - so that you do not find yourself a "stateless" person, "the man without a country." A person without a passport and a nationality is legally lost in this world of national borders and customs officials - and as such is not entitled to the legal protection of any government.

The Wall Street Journal reported in 1995 that one poor soul has been living on a bench in the international waiting area of DeGaulle Airport near Paris for the past two years, while several governments and the U.N. Refugee Commission fight over his nationality!

With no valid passport, international travel is difficult if not impossible, and a person who renounces U.S. nationality must apply for a visa to return to the U.S., just as any other alien does. If found ineligible for a visa, the ex-U.S. citizen can be barred from entering the United States.

Your Right to Leave

Every American has the unconditional power to relinquish his or her United States citizenship. Section 349(a) of the Immigration and Nationality Act (8 U.S.C. 1481) states:

> A person who is a national of the United States whether by birth or naturalization, shall lose his nationality by voluntarily performing any

of the following acts with the intention of relinquishing United States nationality:

. . . .

(5) making a formal renunciation of nationality before a diplomatic or consular officer of the United States in a foreign state, in such form as may be prescribed by the Secretary of State . . .

Valid renunciation must be an unequivocal act in which a person manifests an unqualified intention to relinquish U.S. citizenship. In order for renunciation to be effective, all of the conditions of the statute must be met; the person must appear in person and sign an oath of renunciation before a U.S. consular or diplomatic officer, usually at an American Embassy or Consulate. Renunciations not in the form prescribed by the U.S. Secretary of State have no legal effect. Because of the way in which Section 349(a)(5) is written and interpreted, Americans cannot effectively renounce their citizenship by mail, through an agent, or while within the United States.

Once a renunciation is accomplished before an American diplomatic or consular officer abroad, all documents are referred to the U.S. Department of State. The Office of Overseas Citizens Services reviews them to ensure that all criteria under the law are met, but the State Department has no discretion to refuse a proper renunciation - the personal right to renounce is absolute.

Long before such a drastic final step is taken towards ending U.S. citizenship, the new Canadian immigrant should have his or her official Canadian citizenship in order, papers in hand and an established residence in their new homeland - most likely in Montreal, Toronto or Vancouver where the vast majority of immigrants decide to live.

Essential Preliminaries

The Immigrant Offshore Trust

The key to eligibility for this unusual, Canadian tax-free "window of opportunity" for wealthy Americans willing to surrender U.S. citizenship and become Canadian citizens is found in section 94(1) of Canada's Income Tax Act of 1952 ("the Act").

In essence, section 94 ensures that an immigrant who has never been a Canadian resident can live in Canada and earn tax-free foreign source income from a non-resident trust or affiliated corporation, for the first five calendar years of the immigrant's Canadian residency.

For planning purposes, Canadian residency should begin not in January, but in December of the first year of residency, so that the person will benefit from five full calendar years - 60 months - of tax freedom. The law grants this privilege for all or part of the first five calendar years of residency, not for five years from the first date of residency.

The Beneficiary

To qualify for this big tax break, the arrangement must include:

(a) an immigrant person resident in Canada, and either

(b) a foreign corporation or a trust (wherever located) with which the person in Canada is "closely tied" (meaning, according to court decisions, "not dealing at arm's length"), or

(c) a foreign affiliate corporation controlled by a person resident in Canada, as defined by law (about which we will have more to say later).

The essential factor is that the non-resident trust must have one or more beneficiaries who are Canadian residents, or the offshore corporation must be "closely tied" in some manner to one or more Canadian residents.

The beneficiaries likely will be your family members, and can include yourself. The foreign trustee will follow your instructions on how the trust assets should be invested and income disbursed. Except for the distance involved, you will notice very little difference in your financial operations.

Under Canada's revenue laws (subsection 248(25) of the Act) a "beneficial interest" in a non-resident trust is defined as belonging to a person or partnership that holds any right - immediate or future, absolute or contingent, conditional or otherwise - to receive any of the income or principal capital of the trust, either directly or indirectly.

It would be difficult to find a broader definition of "beneficial entitlement" than this - and the implications for tax avoidance are obvious and potentially enormous.

What's more, Canadian tax officials and court cases have repeatedly stated that such "immigration trusts" and related businesses, when properly created and managed abroad, are not an abuse of the tax laws, because section 94 clearly is designed as a vehicle for exempting new immigrants from taxation for the stated period of five years. In the case of almost every other tax-avoidance scheme, Revenue Canada would pounce. Here the law does more than permit tax avoidance, it approves and encourages it.

Only a change in Canadian law by Parliament could remove this generous tax break, and there is no current talk of removing a provision that has been so successful in attracting needed capital and business to the nation.

Trust Property Sources

In order for a non-resident trust or a non-resident corporation that qualifies as a "controlled foreign affiliate" to receive section 94 tax-free treatment, it must have acquired its property (which, note carefully, can include guaranteeing or making a loan to the trust or company) from a particular person who meets all of the following requirements:

a) the donor must be the trust or affiliate corporation beneficiary, or related to the beneficiary (spouse, child, parent), or be the uncle, aunt, nephew or niece of the beneficiary;

b) the donor must have been resident in Canada at any time in an 18-month period before the end of the trust's first taxation year or before his or her death;

c) if the trust property came from an individual, the individual donor eventually must be a resident in Canada for a period or periods totalling more than sixty months.

Section 94 applies regardless of the method by which the non-resident trust or corporation acquires its property including purchase, gift, bequest, inheritance or exercise of a power of appointment by or from an individual. The law treats all such transfers as if the donor had transferred his or her property to the trust or corporation.

There are some restrictions on the donor to an offshore trust that must be carefully avoided. The donor cannot retain any reversion right or power to designate beneficiaries after the trust is created - this is what is known as an irrevocable living trust. He or she cannot retain any control over how the trust property will be disposed of during the donor's lifetime. If the property is donated to an offshore corporation, the donor cannot retain any greater interest in the company than a 10 percent equity ownership.

As a general rule a trust donor should transfer only cash and title to intangible assets (stocks, bonds, etc.) to an offshore trust. Portable assets, such as gold coins or diamonds, also can be used.

Title to real estate or a business located in Canada or the United States definitely should not be made a part of the trust property. Transfer of tangible property physically located in either nation does nothing to keep those assets away from Canadian or American creditors or tax authorities, and could subject the trust to the jurisdiction of a Canadian court. By holding title to assets within Canada, the offshore trust could be deemed to be doing business in Canada and therefore liable for Canadian taxes.

Foreign Control A Must

In order to determine if an offshore trust is "non-resident" from a tax perspective, Revenue Canada looks to the incidents of control and ownership.

The residence of a trust by ascertaining where the managing trustees or the persons who control the trust assets actually reside. It is therefore important that the offshore trust have a majority of trustees living in the foreign jurisdiction where the trust is registered and where its operation is located.

This requirement for majority offshore control does not diminish the ability of a trust beneficiary to serve as a trustee, and to live in Canada. Neither status jeopardizes the offshore, and therefore tax-free, status of the trust.

Canadian tax law specifically allows offshore immigration trusts to receive tax-free income from investment business conducted by a Canadian citizen living in Canada during the five-year residency period required under section 94.

Thus the new Canadian investor-citizen is free to roam the world by phone, fax, telex, wire, courier or letter, using his capital and ability to produce profits for the trust and its beneficiaries. But to maximize tax avoidance, the trust should not carry on other active business in Canada or invest in property located in Canada, sale of, or income from which otherwise may subject the trust to certain domestic taxes because of the Canadian source or location.

Creating an Offshore Immigration Trust

When creation of an offshore trust is considered, whether for Canadian tax purposes under section 94, for general asset protection, or to shift and shield income from high taxes in the trust donor's country of residence (wherever that may be), a tax haven country is the natural location for sensible trust creation and operation.

With a goal of paying no taxes and/or avoiding taxes at home, one must look abroad for a friendly national jurisdiction in which to locate, a place where little or no taxes are imposed - and where a section 94-qualified enterprise will be legitimate and welcome.

Although it wasn't always so, today a foreign trust located in a tax haven nation is an internationally established and proven fixture in effective offshore financial planning. This type of trust is the safety vehicle that places personal assets beyond the reach of many irritants: your native taxing authorities, potential litigation plaintiffs, an irate spouse or unreasonable creditors, where ever such opponents may be located.

Even though an offshore immigration trust can guarantee five tax-free years for the new Canadian citizen, some of the most important advantages are the non-tax benefits. To other Canadian citizens ineligible for section 94 status, the asset protection benefits of an offshore trust can be far more valuable than potential tax savings, although those are also available. Having such a trust allows Canadians not only the protection of their assets from creditors, but a high degree of financial privacy, flexible estate planning and the ability to engage in international and diversified investments unrestricted by domestic Canadian law.

Many wealthy Canadians today have at least one financial foe they fear more than Revenue Canada - an irate plaintiff's lawyer. As in the U.S., business and professional people too often suffer at the hands of a legal system with judges eager and willing to give others peoples' assets to a sympathy-inspiring plaintiff. One mistake, one unfortunate accident, can take away the fruits of life's labors, and insurance companies often cannot or will not cover fully liability claims. The offshore trust can do the protective job when others won't.

Because of this, many successful professionals and business owners are putting a higher priority on asset preservation than on tax avoidance. A foreign offshore trust is an excellent means to preserve one's wealth, a point to remember as the five-year Canadian tax moratorium nears its end.

A Word About Tax Havens

Simply stated, a tax haven is any country whose laws, regulations, traditions, and usually, international treaty arrangements make it possible for any person, trust or corporation, domestic or foreign, to reduce their overall tax burden. This can be accomplished by moving existing operations into the tax haven jurisdiction or by establishing a new legal entity within the country. This general definition, however, covers many types of tax havens, and it is important to understand the differences.

"No Tax" Havens

These are countries with no personal or corporate income, capital gains, or wealth taxes, places where you can easily incorporate a business and/or form a trust. The governments of these countries do earn some revenue from corporations and trusts, imposing small fees on documents of incorporation, a charge on the value of corporate shares and annual registration fees.

Primary examples of such countries are the British Crown Colonies of Bermuda and the Cayman Islands, and the Commonwealth of the Bahamas, an independent nation within the British Commonwealth of Nations.

Consider for example, the Cayman Islands tax structure.

There are no taxes levied except stamp taxes on certain transactions and import duties. Non-residents who form exempted corporations automatically qualify for and receive a government guarantee of no taxes for twenty years; trusts are given a fifty year no-tax guarantee.

The process of incorporation is quick, easy, simple and cheap. It can be done in a matter of hours at the office of the Registrar of Companies in George Town, the capital city located on Grand Cayman Island, only 475 air miles from Miami International Airport.

There is a registration fee and an annual operating fee thereafter. Start up costs will run about $2,500, with a yearly operating cost of about $1,500. Establishing a trust can cost about $1,000. The Caymans corporation and trusts statutes allow a wide range of business activities, stock issues and great flexibility in actual operation.

The Caymans are noted for laws strongly protecting corporate and bank privacy with stiff penalties of fines and prison for any one, including government officials, who violates the law.

Unlike a corporate charter and bylaws, the actual language of a trust agreement is not registered with government authorities in most countries. Some tax haven countries require registering trusts agreements, so you must consider whether this is helpful or harmful from your point of view. In most cases the terms of the agreement are between you and the trustee, unless a dispute forces one of you to bring the trust agreement into court. Many trust beneficiaries have never seen the trust agreements.

Here's how a Canadian can establish a financial base in the Caymans (or some other tax haven):

Let's say you have $3 million you wish to invest, but being a reasonable person, you want to avoid Canadian taxes on the income produced from your investment. The new immigrant has five years of tax freedom, but other Canadians can also use the Caymans to cut taxes.

First you need a non-resident of Canada - a friend or relative to act as manager of your offshore investment corporation which will be registered in George Town - you can't do it yourself, since the new Canadian immigrant must live in Canada for five years. You transfer the $3 million to an offshore Cayman-registered trust, also administered by your friend as trustee, probably in the same George Town office. That money is invested by the trust in Canadian government treasury bills or public company stocks, and the interest income this produces can be paid by the trust to you, your children or other named beneficiaries tax free. At current interest rates that means a savings of about $100,000 a year in taxes.

While this tax haven structure - a Cayman corporation and a trust - may seem expensive to establish, the arrangement qualifies under section 94 for five-years of tax free income for trust beneficiaries. After the five year period ends, this arrangement can continue to shield the Canadian beneficiary from taxes, so long as it is controlled by non-Canadians.

The worst that can happen if Revenue Canada challenges the post-five year operation, is taxation imposed at the rate you would have suffered had you not tried to continue offshore - plus non-deductible interest on the reassessed taxes and a few thousands of dollars in cost for the legal paperwork and registration in the no-tax Caymans. The best possible result will be major tax savings you could obtain in no other way.

"No Tax on Foreign Income" Havens

Countries in this category impose income taxes, both on individuals and corporations, but only on income earned within that country, not abroad. The laws here exempt from tax any income earned from foreign sources involving no local business activities, apart from simple "housekeeping" matters. For example, there is often no tax on income derived from the export of local manufactured goods, since these countries wish to encourage domestic industrial expansion and local jobs.

The "no-tax-on-foreign-income havens" break down into two groups. There are those; 1) that allow a corporation to do business both internally and externally, taxing only the income coming from internal domestic sources; and, 2) those requiring a company to choose at the time of incorporation whether it will do business locally, with consequent tax liabilities, or will do only foreign business, and thus be exempt from taxation.

Primary examples in these two categories are the Republic of Panama, the British colony of Gibraltar and the United Kingdom-associated islands of Jersey, Guernsey, the Isle of Man.

"Low Tax" Havens

Countries in this status impose some taxes on all corporate income, wherever earned worldwide. However, most have international double-taxation agreements with high-tax countries like Canada, that may reduce the withholding tax imposed on income earned in the high-tax countries by the local corporations. Cyprus is a primary example. Barbados is another low-tax country (with a 2.5 percent tax on corporate income) popular with Canadian business people, about which more below.

"Special" Tax Havens

These countries impose all or most of the usual taxes, but either allow valuable tax concessions, write-offs or "holidays" to special types of companies they wish to encourage (such as a total tax exemption for shipping companies, movie production companies, or financial and investment institutions), or they allow special types of corporate organization, such as the highly flexible corporate arrangements offered by the Grand Duchy of Liechtenstein.

The Netherlands and Ireland are particularly good examples of nations which offer major tax concessions to selected foreign businesses.

Ireland - Special Opportunities

Just as with Barbados, the Republic of Ireland can also be used as the location of an offshore corporate affiliate - giving you commercial access to 340 million potential customers who live within the boundaries of the European Community.

Using Ireland as an affiliate base is one way to lock in low labor costs and a 20-year tax holiday in the process. In some cases, you can even get free government money to fund your start-up costs. Irish labor costs are only 60% to 70% of Canadian wage levels, there is a 10% ceiling on corporate taxes, and cash grants are available to lure foreign business investors.

Since the 1970s, the Irish government has pursued an aggressive foreign investment program. To encourage foreign entrepreneurs to set up businesses, the government created the Irish Development Authority (IDA). To qualify for IDA incentives, a company must be engaged either in manufacturing or in international services. The latter category includes computer or software services, offices for insurance companies, and financial and other primary services.

The Irish parliament has passed a law extending through the year 2010 the maximum corporate tax rate of 10% on foreign investments. Thus, Canadian companies investing now can look forward to fifteen years of substantial tax relief. The government cash grants can take the form either of picking up the entire first year's payroll for a labor intensive business, such as software development, or of capital grants for factories or other more capital-intensive operations.

In addition to the IDA program, Ireland offers other programs. One of them is the Shannon Free Zone program. Incentives are similar to those of the IDA, with taxes held to 10% and capital grants available. Companies are required to locate near Shannon Airport. The Shannon Free Zone operation is administered separately from the IDA.

Ireland offers many advantages compared with rival centers such as Luxembourg and the Channel Islands, through lower wage and housing costs, a skilled and abundant labor force and good communications with other European business centers.

One of the IFSC's attractions has been the possibility for cash-rich firms to place their surplus cash in investment funds which are then managed in Dublin by specialist companies. Profits are taxed at the 10 per cent rate and can be repatriated without further tax liabilities due to Ireland's double taxation treaties with its EU partners.

A Need for Caution

The objective of an offshore tax haven is the legal reduction of your tax obligations.

Keep in mind it will do you no good to suffer the bother of restructuring your financial life, only to find yourself embroiled in years of complex and expensive court battles with Revenue Canada. Or worse, finding yourself facing criminal charges for tax evasion, or a variety of other possible tax crimes.

Reasonable caution places a premium on pursuing the correct path from the very beginning in order to qualify for initial section

94 tax-free treatment, and this means the assistance of competent, expert advice from the very start. Cutting corners can only mean you and your financial advisors could be in deep trouble.

The Mechanics of Offshore Business

An Ideal Offshore Location

The country in which your Canadian immigration trust and the managing trustee are located should be, for obvious reasons, a nation with strong financial privacy laws. Most tax haven countries do emphasize such statutory privacy rights.

The ideal places for establishing asset-preservation or tax avoidance trusts are tax haven countries such as Nevis, the Cayman Islands, Jersey, the Channel Islands, and the Cook Islands in the south Pacific, among others. These countries have statutory law tailored to your financial needs.

Trustees are not required to divulge information about assets held by a trust - and cannot be forced by Canadian courts to turn over trust assets to Revenue Canada or other Canadian creditors - unless and until those creditors go through the host country's judicial system at great expense and with a lot of time-consuming effort.

Creation of an offshore immigration or other trust will affect your personal tax return only in that a taxpayer must disclose the existence of an offshore trust on his or her annual federal tax return.

From the wealth protection aspect, creditors must get a court to order you to reveal your tax return and the existence of the trust, and that takes time. If they do discover the trust's offshore location and file a collection suit in the haven country, local laws are hostile to non-resident creditors and the trustee can shift the trust and its assets to another country and another trustee in an emergency. Then pursuing creditors must begin the process all over again.

Many of these foreign jurisdictions do not recognize U.S., Canadian or any non-domestic court orders, and a creditor must retry completely the original claim which gave rise to a Canadian or U.S. court judgment. Under such circumstances, it won't be long before the creditor will want to talk about settling the dispute.

The Trust Advantage

This gives trusts a distinct privacy advantage over corporations.

In every tax haven country at least one person involved in organizing a corporation must be listed on the public record, along with the name and address of the corporation. In most countries the directors must be listed on the original charter, but in a few maximum privacy countries only the organizing lawyer is listed, but even that reference gives privacy invaders a starting point from which to work against you.

With a trust, in most offshore havens, nothing other than its existence is required to be registered - and often not even that fact. The trust agreement and the parties involved do not have to be disclosed, and there is little or nothing on the public record. In privacy-conscious countries, the trustee is allowed to reveal information about the trust only in very limited circumstances.

The country chosen for such a trust must have local trust experts who understand fully and can assist you in your objectives. The foreign local attorney who creates your trust unquestionably must know the applicable law and tax consequences.

Once established, the offshore immigration trust in its basic form can consist of as little as a trust account in an international bank located in the foreign country. Many well established multi-national Canadian banks can provide trustees for such arrangements and are experienced in such matters - but, as an extra level of insulation from government pressure, you might want to consider using a non-Canadian bank.

With today's instant communications and international banking facilities it is as convenient to hold assets and accounts overseas as it is in another Canadian or U.S. city. Most international banks offer Canadian and U.S. dollar-denominated accounts which often have better interest rates than Canadian institutions.

Trust Creation Advantages

Depending on the country of choice, the settlor of an offshore trust can gain many advantages including the exercise of far greater control over assets and income from the trust than permitted under domestic Canadian law.

The trust can provide privacy, confidentiality, and reduced domestic reporting requirements in Canada; avoidance of domestic taxes and probate in case death taxes are reimposed; increased flexibility in conducting affairs in case of disability, in transferring assets, international investing, or avoiding possible domestic currency controls. A foreign trust can also substitute for or supplement costly professional liability insurance or even a prenuptial agreement as protection for your heirs and their inheritance.

Trust Structure

The structure of an offshore immigration trust is not very different from that of a domestic Canadian trust.

The settlor creates the trust by transferring title to his assets to the trust, to be administered by a trustee according to the terms of the trust declaration. Usually the trustee is a bank in the offshore jurisdiction chosen. Beneficiaries can vary according to the settlor's estate planning objectives and the settlor himself, may be a beneficiary under section 94.

Many foreign jurisdictions also permit appointment of a trust "protector" who, as the title indicates, oversees the operation of the trust to insure its objectives are being met and the local law is followed. A protector does not manage the trust, but can veto actions in limited instances.

The greatest worry about a foreign asset protection trust often is the distance between you, your assets and the people who manage them. While your assets do not have to be transferred physically to the foreign country in which the trust exists, circumstances may dictate such a precautionary transfer. Without such a physical transfer, a Canadian court could decide to disregard the trust and take possession of the assets.

When considering a foreign country in which to located your trust you should find out whether local laws are favorable, clear, and offer the certain protection you seek. Check the past economic and political stability of the country, the reputation of its judicial system, local tax laws, the business climate, language barriers and available communication and financial facilities.

Several offshore financial centers have developed legislation hospitable to foreign-owned asset protection trusts, among them the

Caribbean-area nations of Nevis, the Cayman Islands, the Bahamas, Belize, the Turks and Caicos Islands, and the Cook Islands near New Zealand, as well as Cyprus and Gibraltar in the Mediterranean.

Most of these countries have laws preventing foreign creditors from attacking trust assets unless the suit is brought within two years from the date of the trust creation.

The Offshore Corporation

The offshore corporation is best suited for the needs of Canadian business owners who wish to do good business - and also do very well for themselves when it comes to lowering their taxes and increasing profits. Under section 94, "affiliated" offshore corporations qualify as sources of income for the new immigrant granted five-year tax freedom - and the company can be used for tax-avoidance after the five-year moratorium ends, as we explain below.

But foreign corporations, as Revenue Canada demands, must be more than a mere "sham." A full-scale company, complete with working offices, staff, international fax and telecommunications facilities, bank accounts, a registered agent, board of directors, a local attorney and an accountant can cost upwards of $50,000 annually.

Members of your board of directors, associates of the local tax specialists who help you form the company, will be paid about $2,500 a year. There will be annual taxes to pay and reports to be filed with the local government, and with Canada.

As the Canadian owner you will want to visit your company offices once or twice a year, a pleasant enough activity if you locate your business in one of the tropical venues specializing in such corporate arrangements - the Bahamas or the Cayman Islands, for example. January is an excellent month to visit.

How It Works

Let's say as a new investor immigrant you purchase a Canadian manufacturing business exporting $5 million in products around the world each year.

Because you are a legitimate business with established foreign transactions, your Canadian company can incorporate an offshore affiliate in say, Barbados - like Canada, a member of the British Commonwealth, and a place where international companies pay only 2.5 percent corporate income tax - unlike Canada's 45 percent.

There are less than three quarters of a million people living on this pleasant, tropical 166-square-mile island, where the mean temperature hovers between 76 and 80 degrees fahrenheit all year round.

You can set up your affiliate with offices in the capital, Bridgetown (population 8,000), a city with eight major international banks, including branches of the Royal Bank of Canada and the Canadian Imperial Bank of Commerce - as well as Chase Manhattan and Barclays. Regular air service is offered by Air Canada, British Airways and American, among others.

Your Bridgetown affiliate will handle all foreign sales and international marketing for your Canadian company, for its services charging a 15 percent mark-up on the value of the goods it sells, or about $750,000 a year, at your current export levels.

What you have done is legally transfer your Canada profits to your offshore affiliate where taxes are much lower - 2.5 percent vs. 45 percent! After gladly paying $18,750 in Barbados local corporate income taxes, the rest of the money, $731,250, can be sent back to Canada as a dividend from exempt surplus income, paid to the parent company - tax free! And during the first five years of your citizenship, you personally can share in that corporate income tax free!

Even after your five years of tax grace ends, until the parent company shareholders need the money for their own use, or until they sell the business, Canadian taxes on the income can be deferred indefinitely. If the shareholders want payment immediately, it can be paid out as dividends - and taxed by Canada at the rate of 36 percent, well below the personal income tax rate of 50 percent plus.

Investment Potential

The Barbados affiliate could also serve as an investment arm for your parent company, actively making international investments. All the earned income from such investments - dividends, interest and capital gains - will go to your Bridgetown affiliate, and be taxed at the 2.5 percent rate. Investment profits can also be sent to the parent company, tax free. In order to follow this course successfully, meeting the rule requirements laid own by Revenue Canada, all corporate investment decisions must originate with your Bridgetown money manager, who runs your affiliate on a daily basis - it cannot be you dictating every move by phone from Montreal or Ottawa.

As an added consideration, those with experience say that in order to be successful in using foreign affiliates for investment purposes, a minimum of $1 million in initial capital is needed to start.

In theory this all sounds grand, but there are practical problems associated with an offshore corporation.

First of all, just as in establishing a domestic corporation, legal formalities must be strictly observed when you incorporate abroad - Revenue Canada will check this carefully - and, as we said, the cost of starting up can be considerable. You will need a local legal counsel who knows the law and understands your business and tax objectives. Corporations anywhere are rule-bound creatures requiring separate books and records, meetings, minutes and corporate authorizing resolutions which make it less flexible than many other arrangements.

But you can pay for a whole lot of record keeping with the money you can save.

Reliable Sources of Help

Expert Swiss Money Management Assistance

An excellent choice is Weber Hartmann Vrijhof & Partners, an independent Swiss portfolio management firm that can manage your investment account, whether it be an individual portfolio or a portfolio for your offshore trust or corporation.

WHVP builds on the Swiss money management tradition by providing personal, customized and comprehensive international financial consulting and asset management to private and institutional investors. Their work is characterized by an intensive relationship with their clients. Your personal asset manager is available to you at all times to ensure that your individual needs are met. They will assist you in opening an account with one of Switzerland's first-class banks in Zurich, which will be the custodian of your assets.

As you might expect from Swiss money managers, we apply strict and conservative asset management principles. Our highest priority is the preservation of the long-term purchasing power of your capital. Growth and income are achieved via global diversification in assets and currencies. Risks may be hedged with options and other appropriate instruments.

A large percentage of their clients are based in the United States. One of their main goals has always been to get a certain portion of their clients' wealth out of the U.S. dollar and into European hard currencies such as Swiss francs, Deutschmarks, and Dutch guilders. They then build a portfolio with a mix of bonds and shares. They normally buy stocks as a strategic core holding and invest only in blue chip companies.

The senior partners are Robert Vrijhof, René Schatt, and Adrian Hartmann.

The banking career of Robert Vrijhof began in 1978 with the Union Bank of Switzerland, working his way through the international securities trading department. Later, with Credit Suisse, he held the senior position as manager of the Foreign Stock Exchange trading section. In 1987, he accepted an offer by Foreign Commerce Bank as portfolio manager. His profound knowledge in this area soon led to the position of Vice-President and head of the portfolio management group at Focobank.

René Schatt started his banking career in 1977 with the Thurgauer Cantonalbank, where he finished his basic training. In 1984, he joined the Foreign Commerce Bank and worked his way through the securities administration and trading department. At the same time, he continued studying and in 1987, he achieved the "Federal Diploma of Banking Expert." In 1990, he was promoted to Vice-President and head of the securities department. In 1992, he joined the first Korean Bank in Switzerland, KDB Bank (Switzerland) Ltd., working as Senior Vice-

President and being the Swiss Member of the General Management.

The banking experience of Adrian Hartmann began in 1968 with Foreign Commerce Bank in Zurich, followed by senior management positions with Swiss Bank Corporation. In 1978 he moved to Canada to manage their Toronto office, and later spent four years in the Cayman Islands with his own money management firm. From 1985 to February 1992 he managed the North American subsidiary of Foreign Commerce Bank in Vancouver as President and CEO.

They provide a very personal, comprehensive financial service to a select group of private investors. Everything they do is customized to suit the particular needs of their clientele. Their highest priority is the protection of long-term purchasing power.

The minimum amount to set-up an account with this firm is US$200,000 or equivalent. When you are ready to proceed, you can contact:

Weber, Hartmann, Vrijhof & Partners Ltd.
Attn: New Clients Department
Zurichstrasse 110B
CH-8134 Adliswil
Switzerland
telephone: (41-1) 709-11-15
fax: (41-1) 709-11-13, attn: New Clients Department

Michael Checkan, President of Asset Strategies International, Inc. and Editor, Information Line, says "The feedback from clients who started a relationship with Weber Hartmann Vrijhof & Partners has been extremely positive."

The personalized service means one of the team-members will provide regular updates by telephone about the performance and the market situation. It means further that they will make visits to meet with clients at convenient locations.

Swiss Annuities for Asset Protection

Another product that can be included in your trust is a Swiss annuity.

One of the unhappy facts of financial life in a lawsuit-happy society such as the United States is the increasing danger of being sued. And if you should have the misfortune to wind up on the receiving end of some courtroom debacle, it could easily cost you your life savings.

One of the best ways to protect yourself against such a calamity is to invest in a vehicle that will be beyond the reach of North American courts. One such vehicle is a Swiss annuity.

Swiss annuities can even be used to shield assets from a bankruptcy proceeding. That is because the rights of an insured U.S. person subscribing to a Swiss annuity policy are deemed to be located at the domicile of the Swiss insurance company -- that is, Switzerland, not the United States.

Even if a U.S. court specifically orders the seizure of assets in a Swiss annuity -- or orders that they be included in, say, a bankruptcy settlement -- such an annuity will be protected under Swiss law.

The only way a creditor can seize such an annuity is if the purchase of the policy -- or the designation of the beneficiaries -- is found to be a fraudulent conveyance under Swiss law.

Fraudulent conveyance takes place only: (1) if the insured person bought the policy or named the beneficiaries less than six months before the bankruptcy decree was issued -- or six months before some other collection action; or (2) if the insurance policy was bought or the beneficiaries chosen with the clear intent of damaging creditors.

Of course, such intent cannot be proven if the policy was purchased and the beneficiaries named at a time when the insured person was solvent or when no creditors claims were outstanding. Nor can it be proven if your policy is not written for an excessively large sum relative to the insurance needs of your family.

Another item that can make an important difference in the amount of asset protection a Swiss policy provides is the designation of beneficiaries. Beneficiaries may be named on a revocable or irrevocable basis.

As long as your beneficiary is your spouse, it doesn't matter whether he or she is named on a revocable or irrevocable basis. In either case, your asset protection remains intact.

However, if your beneficiary is a third party (that is, neither a spouse nor a descendent), the designation must be made on a irrevocable basis. If not, the policy can be seized by a creditor.

Note that an annuity or life insurance policy can involve up to four parties, each of which can be in a different country or jurisdiction. The four parties are:

1) the insured individual. If he is not the policy owner, he does not have any rights. When he dies, the contract matures and benefits are paid to the beneficiaries.

2) the policy owner or policyholder. He chooses the policy options and designates the beneficiaries who are paid upon the death of

the insured person. The policyholder may be an individual, a corporation, or a trust.

3) the beneficiaries. These may be individuals, corporations, or trusts. However, if asset protection under Swiss law is your concern, your beneficiaries should only be individuals -- preferably your spouse and/or children.

4) the premium payer. This may safely be an individual, corporation, or a trust.

Note that a properly written Swiss annuity policy affords better protection than Swiss bank accounts -- or Swiss securities accounts. Swiss life insurance policies also make great estate-planning vehicles -- regardless of the risk of bankruptcy or asset seizure.

If you would like more information, an excellent Swiss insurance broker dealing with North American clients is NMG-IFS International Financial Services, providing independent professional financial services. The NMG Group was originally formed as an actuarial consulting and related financial services company in Singapore in 1991. Today, NMG has become the largest provider of financial services consulting in Asia, and has established itself as a market leader in specialist advice on emerging economies. NMG now has consulting operations and representation in 18 cities on six continents.

NMG International Financial Services Ltd. is a subsidiary of the NMG Group domiciled in Zurich, Switzerland. It is an independent investment consultancy firm established to satisfy the investment and financial protection needs of international clients. They do this by selecting outstanding Swiss and international insurance and banking products while offering exceptional advice and service.

Their services include:

- Asset Protection Strategies
- Fixed, Variable, or Private Annuities and Endowments
- Portfolio Bonds
- Life insurance
- Bank Accounts
- World Class Portfolio Managers

Their investment solutions take in account global investment theories and strategies and individual and local investment requirements including tax advantages, asset protection and estate planning. Our worldwide network, experience and know-how enable us to select first class investment solutions through insurance companies, banks and international law firms and to

combine them to form one perfectly fitting solution.

As a one-stop source they take care of everything for you. They provide full sales and after sales services and deal on your behalf with banks, insurance companies and other service providers all over the world.

More information may be obtained from:

NMG International Financial Services Ltd.
Goethestrasse 22, Suite 5
CH-8001 Zurich
Switzerland
Telephone +41-1-266 21 41
Fax +41-1-266 21 49   Please mark fax "Attn: Suite 5"

or by completing the Internet inquiry form at http://www.swissinvesting.com/nmg/

Also include a clear explanation of your financial objectives and whether the information is for a corporation or individual or both. You might also wish to include the possible dollar amount that you would be interested in investing.

Portfolio Bonds for Asset Protection

The most popular way of investing funds offshore is still the opening of a managed or unmanaged bank account with a bank located in a favorable offshore jurisdiction. In general, this is done either by directly purchasing individual shares with the bank, or through an offshore trust.

Rather unfamiliar to many offshore investors is an investment structure called Offshore Portfolio Bond (also known as Private Portfolio Bond, Offshore Insurance Bond, and others).

This investment vehicle combines the best of two worlds - banks and insurances: It is a professionally managed offshore bank account with the benefits of both, a traditional offshore trust and an offshore insurance investment.

The Portfolio Bond can be considered as a simple holding structure. Usually it's domiciled in an offshore tax haven, through which the investor (or his/her selected bank or adviser) can direct the insurance company to invest in a wide range of investment vehicles such as shares, unit trusts, cash deposits, bonds etc.

How it works

The investor closes a contract in his name with an offshore insurance company. He selects a bank and transfers the money to the insurance company's account at that bank. He receives a policy from the insurance company.

Legally the investor is the client of the insurance company and the insurance company is the client of the bank. As the insurance company's client the investor can keep full control of his assets.

According to his instructions, the money will be managed by the bank, an investment manager of his choice (such as Weber, Hartmann, Vrijhof & Partners discussed in the

Why Invest Abroad? chapter) or by himself. In fact, an Offshore Portfolio Bond is a life insurance or an annuity policy. Its value consists precisely in the assets placed there by the life insurance company on the investor's behalf. The money now grows as managed.

Overview of benefits

Besides the important benefits of an offshore account with a private bank (confidentiality, individual asset allocation and strategy, personal care) a Portfolio Bond provides substantial additional benefits.

Separate estate planning

A Portfolio Bond allows to make distributions separate from your ordinary estate and to designate as beneficiary whoever you may wish. However, depending on the policy owner's home jurisdiction some compulsory portions of legal heirs might be reserved.

Upon your death the insurance company will transfer the money to the beneficiaries within 5 days after receipt of the death certificate.

No power of attorney, no last will and no certificate of inheritance are required. Your beneficiaries get immediate access to the money and it will be paid out according to your wish (e.g. lump sum or annual payments).

Asset Protection

Properly structured and established in the right jurisdictions, Portfolio Bonds enjoy legal protection from creditors and cannot be seized or be included in any bankruptcy proceeding. The asset protection comes from the insurance part in your Portfolio Bond.

In some jurisdictions the law is very strict and the protection rock solid. If properly structured, your money is protected even if there is a judgment or court order against you. This major advantage is of particular interest to professionals, or anyone who is exposed to possible lawsuits, malpractice cases, nervous creditors or vengeful ex-spouses.

Confidentiality and privacy

In some jurisdictions, an offshore Portfolio Bond is not just secret and discreet, but protected by law. In Liechtenstein, for example, there is an insurance secrecy law analogous to the banking secrecy law in Switzerland.

Furthermore, offshore insurance companies are strictly confidential and communicate exclusively with the owner of the policy. No information is provided to any third party (natural person or legal entity).

Tax advantages

Unlike many other offshore investments, Portfolio Bonds are, in some jurisdictions, completely free of local taxes. No taxes are due if purchased in offshore jurisdictions like Switzerland or Liechtenstein.

As far as income, capital gains and estate tax are concerned, the law of the investor's tax domicile is decisive.

In various countries insurance policies enjoy substantial tax benefits if correctly structured. Portfolio Bonds offer utmost flexibility and can be tailor-made to fit the legal requirements for tax privilege.

Insurance coverage

Depending on your needs and requirements for your heirs you can add insurance coverage to your portfolio in the event of your death. The amount of insurance can be chosen from zero up to whatever your requirements are and it can also be adjusted during the term of the contract.

This can be very important if a remaining spouse is forced to pay off a mortgage or if heirs need cash to buy out business partners.

More information may be obtained from:

NMG International Financial Services Ltd.
Goethestrasse 22, Suite 5
CH-8001 Zurich
Switzerland
Telephone +41-1-266 21 41
Fax +41-1-266 21 49   Please mark fax "Attn: Suite 5"

or by completing the Internet inquiry form at http://www.swissinvesting.com/nmg/

Further information about NMG is in the Swiss annuities section above.

Afterward

When Five Years End

When the five year residency requirement of the new Canadian citizen nears its end, the offshore trust can either be converted to a domestic Canadian trust (by passing majority control to trustees who reside in Canada), or its affairs can be terminated and the assets distributed to the beneficiaries, in which case they will owe Canadian capital gains taxes on the fair market value at the time of distribution.

That's not a very attractive prospect because the 1995 federal budget eliminated the previous $100,000 capital gains tax exemption.

Once an offshore trust is converted into a domestic trust, its income will be taxed at a rate that varies in each province, but, as we have noted, generally is in the brutal range of 45 to 55 percent.

As for income taxes, Canadians earning US $43,000 and up are taxed on individual income at the top rate ranging over 50 percent, and, as we have pointed out, the tax on corporation income is now as high as 45 percent. The highest effective combined federal-provincial personal income tax rate in 1994 was in the province of Ontario at 52.35 percent.

All of which means you might well plan for residency elsewhere after your five-year, tax-free moratorium expires. We repeat, Canada has no estate taxes and does not levy income taxes on its citizens who live abroad, except on income earned in Canada or assets located within Canada.

Other options include the Swiss annuities and portfolio bonds discussed above, as they may continue to offer tax deferral after the trust is dissolved. Remember that it is also necessary to try to project future tax law changes, so advice given today may not be meaningful five years later. However, insurance products like these may well have at least some deferral possibilities, and one should consult an expert.

Foreign Attractions

After five years of no taxes it won't be easy to face the music of Revenue Canada, especially comparing the outrageously high Canadian income taxes with those imposed in tax haven foreign countries - where, as we have seen, rates for income and corporate taxes are in the low single digits. Prudent Canadians, even if they are not new immigrants, can take advantage of this wide international tax disparity by establishing an offshore tax shelter that can easily double after tax disposable income.

This can be accomplished in full compliance with federal law and the tax code - so that Revenue Canada cannot mount a successful challenge, though based on recent history, RC may well go after anything they consider "overly aggressive tax strategies."

Aggressive Tax Enforcement

The most dangerous attitude one can adopt when dealing with the establishment of offshore business arrangements is the cavalier approach - the idea that "white collar" crimes are somehow less serious than violent crimes, like bank robbery; or the notion that the federal government is less concerned about tax or financial offenses than they are about other civil wrongs.

And don't think geographic distance offers any sure protection for those who want to bend the law by going offshore. During the last fifteen years, Canada has rapidly expanded its tax treaty relations - bilateral and multilateral - aimed at both tax avoidance and tax evasion. Canada now has more than sixty mutual tax agreements in force, or under negotiation with foreign governments.

Canadian courts display a stiff attitude towards tax scofflaws, and the judicial long arm reaches across oceans. For example, the Canadian Supreme Court in Robert Spencer v. R,

85 DTC 5446, held that the former manager of the Freeport branch of the Canadian Royal Bank could be forced to give testimony at a tax evasion trial in Canada, even though doing so would be a breach of the Bahamian bank secrecy law.

The federal government and Revenue Canada's vigorous international tax enforcement efforts have been aided by new and powerful laws aimed at tax avoidance practices. Laws were changed to extend the statute of limitations on government questioning of certain offshore tax transactions from three to six years; RC was given greatly increased powers to obtain "foreign-based information or documents" about a Canadian citizen's business activities abroad; and elaborate, detailed annual corporate reporting requirements were imposed on "intercompany transactions" between Canadians and any offshore affiliated entities. Failure to report or false statements concerning such transactions can cause fines of up to $24,000.

Revenue Canada keeps an eagle eye on the tax shelter industry, and tracks the offshore business activity of individual Canadians, as best it can. Whether RC employing its own informational sources finds out about offshore activity or not, reporting requirements concerning foreign investments squarely place personal responsibility on taxpayers to reveal what they are doing abroad - or suffer the legal consequences if they get caught for not reporting.

In spite of these tough federal tax enforcement policies and an array of laws with sharp teeth, there are still many lawful opportunities for offshore financial activities designed to minimize the impact of Canada's high tax rates. Offshore tax havens are legal, and in selective circumstances there are useful ways in which non-resident owned international investment and business structures can serve you by reducing substantially your exposure to the high taxes of Canada.

Tax Shelters Under Siege

With the exception of the section 94 immigrant trust, Parliament in recent years has "cracked down" on tax shelters, particularly those operating domestically, and this approach includes the 1988 adoption of the infamous "General Anti-Avoidance Rule"or "GAAR," for short.

This radical rule gives Revenue Canada the discretionary retroactive power to revisit and recharacterize for increased taxation purposes, any business transaction which RC interprets as having no "bona fide purpose" - other than to effect a tax savings.

This places squarely on business the burden of demonstrating a "bona fide purpose," (other than tax saving) in order to obtain that savings - and as you might imagine, there have been more than a few court cases contesting the rule's application, scope and still unsettled meaning. That this Draconian rule even exists should give you an accurate idea of the essence - and the direction of federal tax policy.

Before you get nervous, you should know Revenue Canada has ruled that the GAAR specifically does not apply to the tax-free, five-year immigration trusts authorized under section 94.

Strangely enough, the anti-tax shelter government attitude generally does not extend to other offshore tax entities, still governed for the most part by the "Foreign Affiliate System" statute of 1972. This law allows plenty of room for international tax planning designed to minimize domestic taxes by using Canadian-foreign affiliate company profit sharing and dividend distributions.

Offshore Shelter for You?

No one, probably including Revenue Canada, knows for sure how many Canadians now have established - or are about to establish - some form of offshore tax shelter.

But there definitely has been a rush of offshore-bound taxpayers, as indicated by booming attendance at tax haven seminars, sales of books on the subject - and the number of foreign bankers suddenly seeking Canadian business. Every increase in the tax rates means another layer of upper income taxpayers finds it affordable to recoup their tax losses by setting up an offshore tax savings mechanism.

As we have noted, among the several foreign jurisdictions that are popular tax-shelter destinations for Canadians are Barbados, the Cayman Islands, the Turks and Caicos - all sunny Caribbean favorites, and European choices including Ireland, the Netherlands and the Channel Islands. All of these foreign bailiwicks have exceptionally low tax rates on corporate and personal income earned by foreign nationals, as well as other attractions to make them economically feasible for offshore Canadian operations.

As we have already said, going offshore is not cheap. Start-up and annual operating costs can be considerable, depending on the form of shelter employed. Before you decide, these costs must be realistically calculated against tax savings and other expenses - including the possible need to defend your tax shelter against attack by Revenue Canada. But if you can cut your taxes by half, that should finance much of your initial cost, and after that the net results will be like receiving an annual bonus.

Tax Haven or "Sham"?

There are four very basic rules of the game concerning offshore tax shelters laid down by Canadian law - and strictly enforced by Revenue Canada.

These rules apply to any offshore tax shelters - either corporations or trusts, including the immigrant trust - and are aimed at abuse of such operations.

1. Residence. A corporation or a trust, even though created in a foreign country under that country's laws, whose effective management is in Canada, will be taxed on its entire income and capital gains as if it were resident in Canada. This goes for a section 94 immigration trust as well.

To avoid this rule, actual control and management must be located within the foreign country, and all legal formalities supporting this status must be observed. A Canadian citizen is not prevented from being a shareholder, officer or director of an offshore company under this rule - but proven majority foreign control, on paper and in fact, is essential.

2. Artificiality. Except in the case of an immigrant trust, there must be a demonstrably credible reason for the operations of the corporation or trust in the foreign country - other than mere tax avoidance. Otherwise Revenue Canada will hold it to be a "sham" and impose taxes as on any Canadian resident. This means there must be a legitimate purpose, a functioning business, a board of directors, an office and staff and all the other trappings of corporate life.

When there is a legitimate business purpose, there will be no Canadian taxes on any income from a corporation based in a tax haven country, until it is actually paid to the Canadian resident in the form of salary or dividends. There is no penalty for accumulation of capital in the foreign company, and no rules which require its distribution.

This means that until the Canadian owner needs money for his or her use, or until they sell the foreign business, taxes on these earnings can be deferred indefinitely - even for decades. Owners who want the money right away can be paid dividends, on which the Canadian tax is 36 percent, well below the income tax rate of 50 percent plus.

It is worth underscoring that if a Canadian corporation has a foreign affiliate company in a country where Canada has a reciprocal tax agreement (nearly sixty nations are now listed by RC), any dividends paid out of the affiliate's exempt surplus (essentially meaning profits from current income), will be tax free if paid in Canada to a corporate shareholder.

94

For example, a foreign affiliate located in Ireland, manufacturing for export to the United Kingdom, and enjoying a tax holiday under liberal Irish business incentive laws, or a Barbados, Cyprus or Jamaican foreign affiliate qualifying under the domestic tax incentive laws of those nations - can easily generate surplus dividends not taxable in Canada to a Canadian corporate shareholder - a major and very profitable tax savings in many instances.

Dividends paid by a tax haven affiliate company to a Canadian corporate shareholder are treated as exempt surplus and are tax free to the Canadian company - a major boon for tax planning and tax reduction. Interest and royalties paid between two such affiliated companies are also tax free.

For example, loan interest paid by a U.S. affiliate to a Canadian company is subject to a 15 percent gross tax - but the same U.S. payment routed through a Netherlands Antilles affiliate corporation to its Canadian affiliate company, would be tax free. It is worth noting in this regard that Canada does not tax foreign affiliates which are in fact holding companies.

3. "FAPI": In order to regulate offshore financial activity by individual Canadians, in 1976 the federal government promulgated the "Foreign Accrual Property Income" rules - known fondly to Revenue Canada and accountants as "FAPI". The FAPI bottom line requires reporting on income tax forms any "foreign accrual property income," especially "passive" income from offshore investments of any kind.

This is so, even if the income is not transferred back to Canada, even if the money only accumulates abroad in a foreign trust or corporate account. Depending on the applicable provision of law, such foreign income may or may not be taxable - but regardless of any tax liability, every dollar of it must be reported.

Personal foreign accrual property income not only must be reported, but certain types of FAPI (as defined by law) from a Canadian-controlled foreign corporate affiliate, and from certain specified foreign trusts, is taxable currently to Canadian shareholders or trust beneficiaries, whether or not that income is actually remitted to Canada. This covers Canadian investors, regardless of how many shares they own, who have passive interests in offshore investment corporations. While the entire actual net profit of the offshore investment company is not taxed proportionally to each shareholder, there is a complicated RC formula which apportions annual tax liability.

Together with annual FAPI reporting requirements, this annual offshore investment tax has dampened Canadian enthusiasm for foreign ventures devoted solely to producing investment income. Again, FAPI does not apply to a qualified immigrant trust.

4. Inter-company Pricing. Tax haven companies created solely for importing into Canada are subjected to full Canadian taxes. In addition, there can be no overpricing charged by a foreign parent company, for example, for exporting goods from its Canadian subsidiary for international sales. Overpricing has been a

popular but illegal tactic used in an attempt to shift capital from parent companies in high tax Canada to the low tax haven affiliate. RC has gone to court repeatedly to challenge such schemes, albeit with mixed results.

In cases of offshore trading, entailing the activities of a Canadian affiliated tax haven company transferring goods between two other countries, RC authorities always watch very closely - and often conduct annual audits. Even if the tax haven company survives the RC residency and sham tests, it may fail the inter-company pricing regulations, especially if Canada is involved as one leg of the shipping triangle as an importer or exporter. Of course when Canada is "out of the loop," as when a Canadian affiliate company in the Channel Islands is shipping Scottish woolens to Europe, such pricing regulations do not apply - and nether do the taxes.

All this may sound complicated and discouraging but - it can be done!

In Conclusion

There you have it. It may seem a difficult road to travel, but becoming a Canadian citizen investor can save you and your heirs many millions of dollars that would otherwise go directly to the U.S. Internal Revenue Service.

Yes, these savings are predicated on major changes including surrender of your U.S. citizenship, moving your self, your family, and your business to Canada, and possible to another country later on - but the true "bottom line" measured in dollar savings can be enormous.

Most persons of wealth usually have considerable talent, a keen sense of adventure and shrewd judgment when it comes to money. And if such people chose the Canadian immigration route, they will earn and retain a lot more wealth than could otherwise be theirs.

About the Author

Adam Starchild is the author of over twenty books, and hundreds of magazine articles, primarily on business and finance. His articles have a appeared in a wide range of publications around the world -- including *Business Credit, Euromoney, Finance, The Financial Planner, International Living, Offshore Financial Review, Reason, Tax Planning International, Trusts & Estates*, and many more. His personal website is on the Internet at http://www.adamstarchild.com/

Readers of this report may be particularly interested in his book, *Passport to Tax-Free International Living*, available at major retailers such as Amazon.com and Barnes & Noble (BN.com).

www.ingramcontent.com/pod-product-compliance
Lightning Source LLC
Chambersburg PA
CBHW012011190326
41520CB00025B/7508